Superstar Cars

Camaro

Lynn Peppas

🌴 Crabtree Publishing Company

www.crabtreebooks.com

Superstar Cars

Author: Lynn Peppas
Publishing plan research and development:
  Sean Charlebois, Reagan Miller
  Crabtree Publishing Company
Editors: Sonya Newland, Adrianna Morganelli
Proofreader: Molly Aloian
Editorial director: Kathy Middleton
Project coordinator and prepress technician: Ken Wright
Print coordinator: Katherine Berti
Series consultant: Petrina Gentile
Cover design: Ken Wright
Design: Paul Cherrill for Basement68
Photo research: Sonya Newland

Produced for Crabtree Publishing by
White-Thomson Publishing
Photographs:

Alamy: Performance Image: pp. 16-17. **Callaway Cars:** pp. 42-43. **Corbis:** Car Culture: pp. 34-35, 38-39. **Dreamstime:** Andrey Troitskiy: pp. 1, 22-23, 58-59; Wangkun Jia: pp. 5, 8-9; Reynald Bélanger: p. 18; Mel Surdin: pp. 18-19; Dboy Studio: pp. 52-53. **Flickr/Creative Commons License:** Jack Snell: p. 15; Exfordy: p. 17; MSVG: pp. 27; Alden Jewell: pp. 30, 34; Nick Ares: pp. 32, 32-33, 40-41; **Getty Images:** pp. 12-13, 30-31; Time & Life Pictures: p. 6; WireImage: pp. 6-7; ISC Archives: p. 24; Bloomberg: p. 54. © **GM Corp:** pp. 56-57. **iStockphoto:** © Stan Rohrer: cover (car); **Motoring Picture Library:** pp. 28-29, 44-45; **Shutterstock:** Christian Araujo: cover (background); Zoran Karapancev: pp. 4-5; Philip Lange: p. 11; Barry Blackburn: pp. 14-15; Dikiiy: pp. 20-21, 26-27, 39; Kosarev Alexander: pp. 46-47; Left Eyed Photography: 48-49; David Huntley: pp. 53, 55. **Wikipedia:** Sicnag/Creative Commons License: pp. 10-11, 12, 22; Bull Doser: p. 25; Rich Niewiroski Jr./Creative Commons License: pp. 36-37, 40, 47; Shiny Things/Creative Commons License: pp. 50-51; Napolift/Creative Commons License: p. 51; Ifcar: p. 57.

Library and Archives Canada Cataloguing in Publication

Peppas, Lynn
    Camaro / Lynn Peppas.

(Superstar cars)
Includes index.
Issued also in electronic formats.
ISBN 978-0-7787-2101-7 (bound).--ISBN 978-0-7787-2106-2 (pbk.)

    1. Camaro automobile--Juvenile literature. I. Title.
II. Series: Superstar cars

TL215.C33P46 2012   j629.222'2   C2012-902283-7

Library of Congress Cataloging-in-Publication Data

CIP available at Library of Congress

Crabtree Publishing Company

www.crabtreebooks.com   1-800-387-7650

Printed in the U.S.A./052012/FA20120413

Published in Canada
Crabtree Publishing
616 Welland Ave.
St. Catharines, Ontario
L2M 5V6

Published in the United States
Crabtree Publishing
PMB 59051
350 Fifth Avenue, 59th Floor
New York, New York 10118

Published in the United Kingdom
Crabtree Publishing
Maritime House
Basin Road North, Hove
BN41 1WR

Published in Australia
Crabtree Publishing
3 Charles Street
Coburg North
VIC 3058

>> Contents

Chapter 1

Camaro Answers the Call »»»

The Chevrolet Camaro first hit the streets in 1966. General Motors had a lot of catching up to do—the Ford Mustang, released two years earlier, was bringing in record-breaking sales. American consumers were ready for sporty looking four-seater cars that were reasonably priced and could still fit a young family. The Camaro was GM's answer to the call.

Against the odds

The Chevrolet Camaro has been cruising American streets for over 45 years. This classic American beauty has stood the test of time and has faced many problems over the years.

These include an energy crisis, the environmental crisis, and America's fascination with the SUV (Sport Utility Vehicle), which threatened the survival of the Camaro.

■■➡
From its early days to the newest models, the Chevrolet Camaro has set the benchmark for American **pony cars**.

Ford's runaway pony car

The Ford Mustang, released in 1964, set a sales record that has not been broken yet. During its first two years, the Mustang sold over one million cars. GM could only watch from the sidelines as Ford's runaway Mustang took the lead. GM scrambled to develop its own pony car that could go head to head with the gaining popularity of Mustang.

America's love affair

The Camaro's darkest year came in 2002, when it seemed that the popular car had run its course with American buyers. Sales were low and it appeared there was no way back. As it turned out, the Camaro's day was not yet done. It made a big comeback in 2010, with updated stylings that still reflected the early years of the model's design. Americans have fallen in love with Chevrolet Camaro all over again.

The 1967 Camaro badge proudly announced its relationship with Chevrolet.

🏁 AMAZING FACTS

Chevrolet and GM

Chevrolet – the car company that makes Camaro – is actually a division of General Motors (GM). GM bought the company back in 1918. It later bought other auto companies such as Pontiac, Cadillac, and Hummer, although some of these were sold off in 2009.

5

The search for a name

Just a few months before it went on sale to the public, GM's answer to the pony car still had no name. Behind the scenes it was called the F-car, or the F-body. The "F" doesn't stand for anything—it was just a random letter chosen by the company. The F-car had tried on the names of different animals for size, such as Panther, but Chevrolet worried that these were too aggressive. GM wanted the name to begin with "C" as many of their other successful car lines did, including Corvette.

Making friends

Eventually, two Chevrolet **executives** called Bob Lund and Ed Rollert got together to think of a name using a 1935 Heath's French to English dictionary. Lund came across the word "camaro" and found that it meant "friend." It sounded like a winner, and the search for a name came to an end.

The head of Chevrolet, Elliott M. Estes, sits in one of the first Camaros in 1966, as the car went on sale to the public.

Preying on the Mustang

When Chevrolet introduced the brand new Camaro to the automotive press, one reporter asked what the name Camaro meant. Chevrolet told them that a Camaro "was a small, vicious animal that ate Mustangs." This was totally untrue, but it did make for a good joke on Ford's Mustang!

Singing its praises

The true test of something's popularity in America is who is singing about it. Many popular musicians have found the Camaro a source of inspiration for rocking their lyrics over the years. The 1980s punk band The Ramones sang "Go Lil' Camaro, Go" back in 1987. Alternative rock band Weezer sings about a "Yellow Camaro."

The sports car has bling-appeal with hip-hop artists T-Pain and Wiz Khalifa, who sing about the "Black and Yellow" Camaro. Rapper Young Jeezy's Camaro is black with blue stripes. Swinging over to country rock, Rascal Flatts sing about a "Red Camaro," and American rockers Kings of Leon's "Camaro" is black as coal. American pop music can't be wrong—the Chevrolet Camaro is definitely worth singing about.

A red Camaro was **customized** for Rascal Flatts and went on tour with the band.

Chapter 2

Catching up to the Competition

Chevrolet designers—the people who create the exterior or outside style and looks of a vehicle—had the idea to produce a car like the Camaro even before the first Mustang was sold. But GM executives had put this idea on hold because they didn't think the time was right for a sporty, four-seater car. They were proved wrong!

Setting the standard

In 1964, Ford sold over 100,000 Mustangs within its first two months of sales. In fact, Ford could not make the Mustang fast enough, and some car buyers had to wait for delivery of their vehicles. GM had a lot of catching up to do. They decided to go full speed ahead with Chevrolet's answer to the pony car.

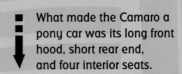

What made the Camaro a pony car was its long front hood, short rear end, and four interior seats.

Camaro's debut

Two years later, the very first 1967 Camaro was unveiled to the American public, on September 12, 1966. There were a lot of different options that people could choose from, but the base price for a Camaro **coupe** was around US$2,400. It was also offeredas a **convertible**, which cost about US$300 more.

Astro Ventilation

The 1967 model was the only Camaro to have side vent windows. By 1968, these windows were replaced with Astro Ventilation. Astro Ventilation was a system that allowed fresh air to enter the car from outside, a job that was normally done by the side vent windows.

Coke bottle design

Coca-Cola has been a "pop" icon in the U.S.A. for over 100 years. Car writers of the 1960s described the exterior lines of the Camaro as having a "Coke bottle design." Turn a bottle of Coke on its side and you can see the resemblance. The center of the bottle has a tucked-in waist, much like the middle of the early Camaros.

9

Upgrade packages

In 1967, car buyers could choose from three Camaro models. The base car was called the Sport Coupe. Upgraded packages included the Super Sport (SS) and Rally Sport (RS) Camaros. Basically, the RS was an **appearance package** with special racing stripes and details. The SS was a **performance package** with larger, faster engines and heavier-duty parts to match the speeds it could reach.

■ The bumblebee nose stripes were first included in the SS version of the 1967 Camaro.

Beauty is only skin deep

SS and RS emblems made it easy to tell the SS and RS edition Camaros apart. The "bumblebee" nose stripe came as part of the SS package. The Camaro RS had electrically operated front headlight covers. Car owners could add RS details to a Camaro SS, so that their automobile would be able to have both the bumblebee stripe *and* covered headlights.

▚ AMAZING FACTS

Tough talking

Camaro designers got the idea for the SS bumblebee nose stripe from jet fighter planes of the day. The idea was to make the front end of the Camaro look a little bit shorter than it actually was— and a whole lot tougher.

The inside story

In the Camaro's first year, three engines were available. The Sport Coupe came as standard with a 3.7-liter, straight-6 (six-cylinder) engine, which had 140 **horsepower (hp)**. This was not a very fast engine. An optional 5.4-liter V8 engine had much more power, and made the driving experience more interesting. Finally, a 5.7-liter big-block V8 with 375 hp was offered as the top-of-the-line engine for all 1967 Camaro SS models.

The SS V8 engine was the peak power offered in the first range of Camaro models.

Camaro's cousin

The Pontiac Car Company, which was also owned by GM, did not want to be left out of the pony-car race. GM executives gave permission for it to take the *platform* of the new Camaro, make changes to it, and sell it as a Pontiac. The Pontiac Firebird came out six months after the Camaro. The only real differences between a 1967 Firebird and a Camaro were in the nose and rear section of the car.

⟩⟩ Muscle car mania

A new trend for car buyers began in the mid-1960s—people wanted muscle cars. Muscle cars are automobiles with huge engines that go extremely fast. In 1967, Camaro's first year of sales, Ford came out with the option for a big-block V8 engine with 320 hp in the Mustang. This made the Mustang "Boss" more powerful than the top-of-the-line small-block V8 that Chevrolet offered in the Camaro. It seemed that the Camaro was still playing catch-up with the Mustang.

Yenko-made Camaros were marked with their own badge.

Yenko Camaro

Don Yenko owned a Chevrolet car dealership in Pennsylvania, and he loved fast cars. He ordered stock Camaros and put in special parts to make them racier vehicles. He replaced the standard engines with L72, V8 big-block Corvette engines. This made them Yenko Camaros, and they came with his signature Yenko emblem.

Muscling in

Chevrolet was determined to not see the Mustang speed by them in sales again and immediately planned what they could do to the Camaro. A few months after its release, in December 1966, two big-block engines were offered for the 1967 Camaro. These were the L35 engine, which was a 6.5-liter V8 with 325 hp, and an even larger powerhouse, the L78, which put out up to 375 hp. These engines helped the Camaro keep up with the other pony cars.

The ZL-1

In 1969, the Camaro ZL-1 was released. On the outside it looked like any other 1969 Camaro, but inside it was a different story. It came with a big-block, seven-liter aluminum-block engine. The engine was lighter so the car could go faster. Chevrolet sold cars such as these under the COPO (Central Office Production Order) program. This program sold specialty car parts, and the ZL-1 Camaro was better suited to a racetrack than a city street.

■ Only 69 Camaro ZL-1s were ever built, and today they are extremely rare and fetch high prices at auctions.

At the races

The SCCA (Sports Car Club of America) held its first Trans-Am racing competition in 1966. One of the classes was a race for factory-manufactured cars, which were cars that anybody could buy from a car lot. The engines in this class could not be over five liters, which put the big-block engines out of the competition. All pony-car manufacturers, including Camaro and Mustang, made a Trans-Am race-ready car in their lineup.

Trans-Am racing series

In 1967, Camaro's Trans-Am racer was a Camaro Sport Coupe with the Z28 option package. This included a 327 V8 engine with a more aggressive handling **suspension**, and 15-inch (38-cm) tires. There were no luxury options offered; this car was definitely made for the racetrack and not for driving around town.

■ The Z28 included broad racing stripes down the length of the hood and trunk, but did not come with a Z28 emblem in its first year.

Vital Statistics

1969 Z28

Production year: 1969
No. built: 20,302
Top speed: 120 mph (193 km/h)
Engine type: V8
Engine size: 4.9 liters, 290 hp
Cylinders: 8
Transmission: Muncie 4-speed
CO_2 emissions: N/A
EPA fuel economy ratings: N/A
Price: US$3,185

Indy 500 pace car

The Camaro was given the honor of pacing the Indianapolis 500 race in 1967. In the 50-year history of the race, the 1967 Camaro was Chevrolet's third pace car. The Camaro SS convertible pace car came equipped with a 396 cubic-inch big-block V8, L35 engine. It was painted Ermine White with blue RS striping and a blue interior.

Chevrolet did not offer a special edition pace car **replica** to car buyers in 1967. But in 1969, Chevrolet was invited to produce the pace car for the Indy 500. This time, a special edition replica pace car went on sale. Over 3,500 people bought one, painted in Dover White with Hugger Orange stripes and orange houndstooth upholstery.

The 1969 Indy 500 pace car replica had distinctive white and orange paintwork.

AMAZING FACTS

Pace car extras

Apart from the three pace cars created for the 1967 Indy 500 racing event, Chevrolet produced 100 similar SS versions that were used to drive sports celebrities for the day of the race. Afterward they were sold as "used" cars.

Chapter 3

▶Camaro Changes for the 70s ▶▶▶

Chevrolet had had enough of trying to catch up to the competition. In 1969, Mustang was still selling more cars than Camaro, although the gap was closing, with Mustang selling 299,824 cars to Camaro's 243,085. Chevrolet felt the time was right for Camaro to pull ahead of the competition with a new, second-generation of the car.

1970½

New cars are usually released in the fall of the previous year—for example, the 1967 Camaro was released in September of 1966. The second-generation's first Camaro was not released until February 26, 1970.

Some people call it the 1970½ because it was half a year behind schedule. There were many changes to the new Camaros—they were bigger and heavier, for a start—and the new design put production of the car behind schedule.

Designers decided to do away with the small, rear side windows altogether. This meant that both the door and the side windows were extra long.

A facelift for the 70s

The nose of the new Camaro was given a facelift, with an inset, V-shaped **grille** and a chrome bumper that divided it lengthwise. It was not very safe, but it was good-looking. The RS package offered the same shaped grille but with two short chrome side corner bumpers instead of just one long bumper.

Placing the plate

The RS nose stuck out even more dramatically because it was surrounded with a body-color **urethane** rim. This presented the problem of where to put the front license plate. On the RS it was placed off to the side, under the car's right front headlight. All other Camaros, the Sport Coupe, Super Sport, and Z28 without the RS package, kept their license plates in the middle where they had always been.

All these changes proved to be a winning combination. Second-generation Camaros were in production for 12 years—a long time in the car world!

Positioning of the license plate proved difficult on the 1970 model because of the large front grille.

Bill Mitchell

Bill Mitchell was GM's vice president of design in 1970. He was best known for his design of famous GM models such as the Corvette Stingray (so-named because Mitchell was a keen fisherman), and the second-generation Camaro. Mitchell drew inspiration for the Camaro from other European sports cars such as the Ferrari.

Changing times

The 1970s brought a lot of changes to the American car industry, and every automaker felt the pinch. Environmental concerns, oil crises, and rising insurance rates changed people's ideas of what kind of cars they wanted to drive. The Camaro kept changing to meet its customers' needs. Chevrolet was determined to offer the best pony car possible for the American car market.

In the 1970s, round taillights began to be a signature feature of Chevrolet cars, including the Camaro and the Corvette.

End of an era

From 1970–72 muscle cars still ruled the roads, but their time was coming to an end. Insurance companies cashed in on the muscle-car trend and raised insurance rates for young drivers with big-block engine muscle cars. The Camaro was offered with its biggest and best big-block engines in 1970, but from then on it was all downhill.

The SS396

A popular big-block engine option for the 1970 Camaro was the SS396. It was actually a 402 cubic-inch engine, but Chevrolet called it the 396 because they thought the numbers sounded better with the SS in front. This car put out a huge 350 hp in the L34 version, and 375 hp in the L78. The Camaro SS was discontinued in 1973.

The 1973 oil crisis

In 1973, the U.S.A. suffered an oil shortage when members of the Organization of Arab Petroleum Exporting Countries (OPEC) placed an oil *embargo* on the U.S. This caused an oil and gasoline shortage in the U.S.A. Suddenly, fuel-efficient cars became much more important in terms of sales, and gas-guzzling muscle cars became a thing of the past.

The SS396 was a high-powered version of the 1970 Camaro SS.

Safety and efficiency

By 1973, the big-block engine was discontinued for Camaro, and all other muscle-car competitors. New **emissions** standards were set by the U.S. Environmental Protection Agency (EPA). As the muscle-car trend ended, a new fashion for safe and fuel-efficient cars began to take its place.

The National Highway Traffic Safety Administration (NHTSA) is the government watchdog agency that sets car safety standards in the United States. The Camaro underwent drastic changes because of the new regulations put into effect to make cars safer.

Bumper cars

In 1974, Camaro redesigned its front and back bumpers to meet the new standards. The Camaro RS's front split bumpers were abandoned. All Camaros came equipped with new aluminum bumpers. Wraparound rear taillights were added to accommodate the bulky back aluminum bumper. Even though these were lifesaving features, the changes were not popular among Camaro-lovers.

The computer age

The 1981 Z28 Camaro got its first ever CCC (Computer Command Control) unit to help it meet the new emissions regulations. In this system, sensors in the car's engine feed information to the computer. The computer controls the engine so that it gets the best performance, while still staying within the emissions standards.

AMAZING FACTS

Limiting speeds

In 1974, the National Maximum Speed Law was posted at 55 mph (89 km/h) on most highways across the U.S.A. It was introduced to cut down on oil and gasoline usage. Since 1995, all states have controlled their own speed limits.

It was impossible to miss the Z28 with its flashy decals, a trademark on this model in the mid-1970s.

Clean Air Act

The Clean Air Act of 1970 was a law passed by the U.S. Congress to control air pollution. It required that all new cars manufactured by 1975 had to cut their emissions by 90 percent. From 1975 onward, all Camaro engines came equipped with a *catalytic converter* that cut emissions and ran on unleaded gas only.

Trading speed for luxury

America's need for speed was quickly swapped for the lap of luxury. Camaros from 1973 onward offered a package with the letters LT instead of RS or SS. It was a whole new ball game for the Camaro. These cars did not have the same brute power as earlier versions, but they did offer a greater variety of luxury options.

Camaro LT

When the Camaro SS was retired in 1972, Chevrolet replaced it with a new model called the Type LT Coupe. The letters LT stand for "luxury touring." The new model was basically an SS, but without an option for a big-block engine. It earned its "L" by providing luxury options such as a tilt steering wheel, wood-grained door and instrument panels, and much more comfortable seats.

The LT models from 1973 onward boasted luxury features such as wood-grained panels on the doors and dashboard.

The Z28 returns

During the mid-1970s, Camaro's distant cousin, the Pontiac Firebird and Trans Am, did not abandon its performance line of cars as Camaro had. Healthy sales of Pontiac pony cars proved that not everyone had lost interest in power over luxury. Chevrolet decided to take a kick at the Z28 Camaro once again in 1977. But instead of speed, the new and improved Z28 would out-handle the best of the sports cars.

Birth of Berlinetta

The Camaro Type LT was given the new name of Berlinetta in 1979. This Type LT Camaro featured an improved suspension system. It was also given more insulation to make it a quieter ride. As an extra option, buyers could order it with the special performance engine—a 350 cubic-inch V8 with 175 hp—that came as standard on the Z28. The Berlinetta was popular with car buyers, but the Z28 was the top seller in the Camaro lineup in 1979.

1977 saw the return of the Z28 performance model. This was also the first year that the Camaro sold more cars than the Mustang!

23

Back to the races

IROC stood for "International Race of Champions," and was a race that was first held in 1973. The competition was between drivers, instead of showing off a car's performance. Each driver was given an identical car to drive in the race. In its first year, drivers were given Porsche Carreras to drive. In 1974, the Porsche was replaced with the Camaro Z28. Chevrolet Camaros were used for the competition for 12 years in a row. The racing event was televised and Chevrolet enjoyed free advertising for its sporty pony car.

Mario Andretti leads the field in his Camaro in the 1979 IROC.

A flare for design

No convertible model was offered in the second-generation. The closest it came was removable glass T-top roof panels first offered in 1978. The same year, a new bumper system was added. The body-colored urethane bumper was not only safer, it changed the Camaro's look, too. In 1979, the Z28 was given new stamped steel wheel rims that were painted the same color as the car.

Sales celebration

Camaro finally managed to outsell its long-time competitor, the Ford Mustang, in 1977. That year Camaro produced 218,853 vehicles. Sales topped 282,571 in 1979—a record that still stands for the Camaro. Sales declined after that. In 1981, only 126,139 were made.

Looking forward

The second-generation, from 1970–81, had been an important time in the evolution of the car. It had been chosen as the official IROC car from 1974. It had met strict safety and fuel-efficiency standards, and had done so without compromising its sporty style and good looks. The second-generation of Camaro was coming near its end by 1981, but a much-anticipated third-generation of Camaro was waiting to be released to the car-buying public.

Vital Statistics

1980 Z28

Production year: 1980
No. built: 45,137
Top speed: 120 mph (193 km/h)
Engine type: V8
Engine size: 5.7 liters, 172 hp
Cylinders: 8
Transmission: Muncie 4-speed
CO_2 emissions: N/A
EPA fuel economy ratings: 14 mpg
Price: US$7,121.32

The 1981 Camaro was the last of the second-generation. It was time for a new look.

Chapter 4
Third-Generation Camaro

The third-generation of Camaro was supposed to be ready for 1980, but Chevrolet needed more time. Finally, in January 1982, the new Camaro was released—late as usual! It was a big hit with car enthusiasts from the start, and lasted for a healthy ten-year span, until 1992.

Camaro gets edgy

The third-generation Camaro made a great first impression with Americans. It looked like a Camaro in that the nose of the car was very long, while the rear was short and chopped-off.

The most obvious change was that the car's body design went from a rounded shape to a more angular design.

Third-generation Camaros had a cleaner, more angular shape. They were also shorter and slightly smaller than earlier generations had been.

Lean machine

The new generation was a lean machine, with a cleaner and classier look than the flashy 1970s models had offered. It also shed noticeable measurements. The new Camaro weighed about 450 pounds (200 kg) less than earlier models. It was ten inches (25 cm) shorter and three inches (eight cm) narrower, too. The third-generation was the first to offer four-speed **automatic transmission** and five-speed **manual transmission**.

Hatchback first

The new Camaro featured a first-time ever hatchback design that is some-times called a third door. The sloping back window was on hinges and lifted up. The hatchback opened from the back of the car. This design made the Camaro more convenient for loading and unloading the cargo or trunk area. In 1982, it was the largest automotive glass part ever manufactured.

The sloping hatchback of the new generation was a first for Camaro.

Gas saver

Another oil crisis in 1979 changed the engines offered in American sports cars even more. Due to the rising price of oil, car buyers in America were looking to purchase vehicles that saved on gas but still looked sporty. The 1982 Sport Coupe was the first Camaro ever to come with a four-cylinder engine as standard. It was a 151 cubic-inch engine offering 90 hp. It looked fast—but it wasn't!

Engine options

Both V6 and V8 engines were optional for Camaros of the third-generation, but for a higher price, of course.

For car buyers who cared more about speed than the price of gas at the pumps, the fastest engine out there for the new generation of Camaro was the 305 cubic-inch V8. This could be ordered as an extra option for the Berlinetta or Z28 Camaros.

Cross-fire injection

In 1982, a cross-fire (fuel) injection system was offered in the Z28. It came with the LU5 version of the V8 engine only. This system injected, or shot, gasoline into the throttle body—a section of the engine's intake system. Gasoline is mixed with air and then used by the engine. Cross-fire injection gave the engine more horsepower—but only when it needed it—and reduced the car's emissions.

The 1982 Z28 was offered with a fiberglass hood which reduced the vehicle's weight.

AMAZING FACTS

Sales record

In 1984, sales of the Camaro went over 260,000. This year's model set the highest sales record for third-generation Camaros, but it still didn't beat the second-generation's top annual sales record of 282,571, achieved in 1979.

Under the hood

The 1982 and 1983 Z28 Camaros came with fiberglass hoods. Fiberglass is a material made from glass fibers surrounded by plastic. It is very **durable**. It is also much lighter than the regular steel that cars are made from. The new hood reduced the Z28's weight.

Give me a brake!

In 1986, the U.S. government introduced a new law that made Center High Mounted Stop Lamps (CHMSL) standard equipment on all new passenger cars, including Chevrolet's Camaro. The new brake light reduced rear-impact accidents. On the Camaro, it was a slim red bar placed on the top of the hatchback window.

Made in the U.S.A.

Third-generation Camaros were made in the U.S.A. at two assembly plants in Van Nuys, California, and Norwood, Ohio. The Norwood plant closed on August 26, 1987. The last car off the assembly line was a Camaro. Full production was carried on at the Van Nuys plant until the fourth-generation Camaro.

Specialty Camaros

In 1985, the Z28 went one better. A new package called the IROC package could be added to the Z28 to make it an IROC-Z. This was the premier performance Camaro, and included a lot of upgrades that took it far beyond the standard Camaro.

IROC-Z rocks!

The IROC-Z Camaro was inspired by the International Race of Champions. The IROC model of Camaro was by far the fastest and sportiest car in IROCs lineup. Camaro had a reputation for being the best handling car on the market at the time. The height of the new IROC-Z was lowered by half an inch (1.3 cm), which made the handling even better. New 16-inch (41-cm) Goodyear Eagle tires improved the car's handling, too. These tires were also standard on the Chevrolet Corvette.

The upgrades offered on the IROC-Z made it a popular performance model.

▟AMAZING FACTS

Gold-medal Camaro

A special edition Camaro Sarajevo Winter Olympics appearance package was sold in November and December of 1984. The cars were painted white with red, white, and blue stripes.

Tuned Port Injection

The fastest engine for the IROC-Z was the LB9 V8, with 225 hp (the highest in a Camaro for more than ten years). It had a new system of fuel injection called "Tuned Port Injection" (TPI). This gave the Camaro better gas mileage and engine performance. The TPI system, much like the cross-fire injection system (CFI), shot a mist of gasoline to mix with air and fuel in the engine. The TPI was even better than CFI, although it only came with a four-speed automatic transmission.

■ To celebrate its 20th anniversary in 1987, the Camaro was made available as a convertible for the first time in nearly 20 years.

20th anniversary

In 1987, Chevrolet celebrated Camaro's 20th anniversary by producing the first convertible Camaros since 1969. The Camaro convertibles were considered to be the anniversary edition. They were made not at a GM plant, but by American Specialty Cars in Southgate, Michigan. In 1987, over 1,000 T-top model Camaros were turned into convertibles.

1LE

When car buyers ordered the 1LE package they were basically getting a racecar. As in previous generations, these were not vehicles to be used for picking the kids up from school or driving to the shopping mall. These were seriously fast automobiles with very few luxury options.

A well-kept secret

Chevrolet offered a rare race-ready Camaro to buyers but kept it secret. This was called the 1LE/G92 package, but it could not be found on the order sheet. Instead, buyers had to check off the exact combination of options to activate the 1LE option. The 1LE

Camaro was such a well-kept secret that only four people ordered one in 1988. Speed enthusiasts were catching on by 1992, and during the last year of third-generation sales, 705 people ordered one. The 1LE package was the fastest Camaro produced from 1988–92.

The B4C was available to the police between 1991 and 2002. In 1992, a package with 1LE brakes and suspension was offered.

Not for just anybody

For most buyers, the 1LE Camaro could not be ordered with air conditioning. However, police forces could order the RPO B4C package with the 1LE Camaro and get air conditioning. Some people convinced dealerships to sell them the B4C package with their 1LE Camaro, even though they weren't supposed to!

Showroom stock

A new SCCA racing class called "showroom stock" was introduced in the late 1980s. Showroom stock is a term used for races that allow sports cars that are ready to race with very few **modifications**.

For Camaro, the 1LE package was created for car buyers looking for showroom stock, race-ready vehicles. Along with powerful engines, showroom stock vehicles needed heavy-duty racing brakes and suspension that could handle the stresses added to a vehicle while racing. 1LE Camaros competed in races in the SCCA (Sports Car Club of America) and in the IMSA (International Motor Sports Association) Firestone Firehawk Series.

Vital Statistics

1988 1LE Camaro

Production year: 1988
No. built: 4
Top speed: 145 mph (233 km/h)
Engine type: LB9 V-8
Engine size: 5 liters, 230 hp
Cylinders: 8
Transmission: 5-speed manual
CO_2 emissions: N/A
EPA fuel economy ratings: N/A
Price: US$14,356

The IROC-Z package was so popular in the late 1980s that it became standard on all Z28 models.

Fast forward

Camaro's third-generation car—with its sharp styling and improved handling—was a hit with American sports-car drivers. It gave more speed using less gas and releasing fewer emissions. What was there not to like? Of course, publicity on and off the racetrack didn't hurt Camaro's sales either.

↑ The 1982 Camaro came in an Indianapolis 500 commemorative model.

Updated pace car

The year in which a new generation of classic sports car such as Camaro is released is always exciting. Camaro's third-generation was no exception. It was chosen to pace the 66th annual Indianapolis 500 on May 30, 1982. The actual pace cars—two of them—were 1982 Z28s, especially equipped with a modified all-aluminum, fuel-injected, 5.7-liter V8 engine.

This engine was not offered on the replica editions. Instead, these came with a standard LG4 five-liter V8. The upper half was painted silver and the bottom half a dark blue. Special blue decals were on the silver upper-side doors and B-frame behind the side window.

Silver anniversary

The third-generation's last year of production was 1992, which was also the year of Camaro's 25th anniversary. Camaro planned to make a special edition car to mark the anniversary but then decided against it. For their silver anniversary, buyers could purchase the Heritage appearance package, which included wide, bold stripes down the length of the hood and rear.

Z28 again

In 1988, the Z28 Camaro was discontinued and replaced by the IROC-Z. Two years later, Camaro lost the rights to use the name IROC-Z when Dodge took over the sponsorship of the International Race of Champions. From 1990 onward, Camaro's performance line was once again called the Z28.

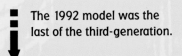

The 1992 model was the last of the third-generation.

Chapter 5
Saving the Best for Last »»»

The fourth-generation of Camaro was released for 1993. Chevrolet gave Camaro buyers fewer model choices. There were no convertibles, although a T-top option could be ordered, and just two models to choose from—the standard Sport Coupe and the Z28. Even though many car enthusiasts felt the new generation was the best so far, Chevrolet officially discontinued the Camaro in 2002.

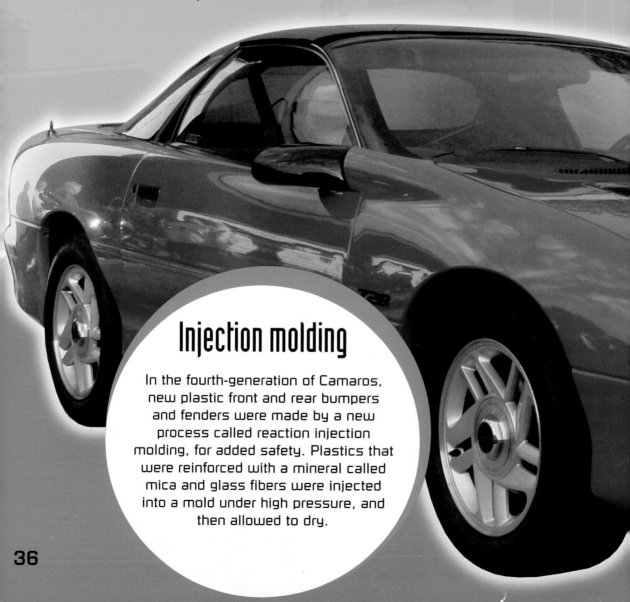

Injection molding

In the fourth-generation of Camaros, new plastic front and rear bumpers and fenders were made by a new process called reaction injection molding, for added safety. Plastics that were reinforced with a mineral called mica and glass fibers were injected into a mold under high pressure, and then allowed to dry.

New look, new materials

The fourth-generation of Camaro looked quite different to the third. The squared-off edges of the third-generation gave way to a rounder, sleeker body. Some people criticized the new look, saying it resembled a Japanese sports car more than an American one. However, the new design had the benefit of making it more **aerodynamic**, which saved on fuel costs.

Size matters

The new generation was a larger car than the generation before it. The Camaro gained half an inch (one cm) in length and almost two inches (five cm) in width. This might not sound like a big difference, but it made the Camaro almost 200 pounds (91 kg) heavier. It would have been heavier yet, but the door, roof, and rear hatch panels were all made of lightweight plastic instead of the usual steel.

The fourth-generation boasted a smoother, sleeker outline and injection-molded bumpers and fenders.

Quality control

The fourth-generation Camaro was considered by many to be the most reliable generation yet. It was known for its superb handling, perky performance, and surprising gas mileage. The previous generation had been criticized, especially in car magazines, for its poor and inconsistent production quality. The fourth-generation seemed to get it just right.

A new face

Jim Perkins grew up in Waco, Texas. One of his first jobs was sorting parts at a Chevrolet warehouse. He worked his way up the GM corporate ladder, but left in 1984. At that time he became senior vice president of the new luxury car brand of Toyota, called Lexus. At Lexus,

Perkins learned the value of producing quality-made vehicles. He returned to Chevrolet in 1989 and, as the company's new general manager, helped develop the fourth-generation Camaro. What Perkins learned at Toyota, he used at Chevrolet, and produced the best generation of Camaro so far.

The fourth-generation of Camaros were praised for their handling and performance on the road.

Made in Canada

In 1993, only 39,103 Camaros were produced. For the first time ever, Camaros were made in Canada rather than the U.S.A., at a plant in Sainte-Thérèse, Quebec. Chevrolet executives were very careful to make sure that the quality of their vehicles was top-notch. Production remained there until August 2002.

Japanese styling

Japanese imports from companies such as Honda and Toyota were a real threat, and cut into American carmakers' sales. The U.S. was being flooded by Japanese cars, and many Americans were no longer buying American-made vehicles. The only thing that was criticized on the new generation of Camaro was that it looked Japanese. But then again, considering the trend toward buying imported cars from Japan, perhaps it was a good thing.

The new generation was widely criticized for looking too much like a Japanese car and not enough like the traditional American automobile.

Speeding ahead

Not only was the new generation of Camaro a sharp-looking and quality-made car, it was also way ahead of the competition in terms of speed. The base Sport Coupe's standard engine was an L32, 3.4-liter V6. The racier Z28's standard engine was an LT1 5.7-liter V8. For those not satisfied with the basic engines, larger options beefed up the speedometer—and the price!

Secret Z28

The 1LE was revived for the fourth-generation of Camaro. This time it came back with the LT1 engines that were offered only in Z28 Camaros. However, car buyers who purchased a Camaro Sports Coupe could order the Special Service Package—the same package used for police vehicles—called RPO B4C. This small-block engine put out 275 hp and could travel at top speeds of 154 mph (248 km/h). It performed like a Z28 but without the Z28 decals, nobody but the driver would know it!

In 1993, the Z28 came as standard with an LT1 V8 engine, although upgrade options were available.

AMAZING FACTS

What's the difference?

It was easy to tell a Z28 apart from other models of Camaro. Fourth-generation Z28s had black roofs whereas base coupes had body-colored roofs. The Camaro convertible also returned as a 1994 model.

Camaro SS returns

SS stands for Super Sport, but it could also stand for sizzling speeds. The SS model of Camaro made a comeback in 1996. The special performance name for Camaro had been last used 24 years ago, in 1972. The new Camaro SS cars were the highest-performance Camaro available at the time.

They were basically 1996 Z28s with an LT1 engine that was modified further with a **turbocharger**, by a company called Street Legal Performance (SLP). The SS was also given a special scooped hood and 17-inch (43-cm) tires that came as standard on 1996 Corvettes.

■ The basic 1996 Z28 was given a turbocharger to turn it into the SS version.

Callaway Camaro C-8

The Callaway Camaro C-8 is an **aftermarket** Camaro that was first produced in 1993 by Callaway Cars. Although it was still a Camaro, the looks and performance made it an entirely unique sports car.

There were two Callaway aftermarket editions of Camaro. The SuperNatural Camaro C-8 was strictly an upgraded performance vehicle. It was given a SuperNatural 383 engine, a V8 beast that put out 404 hp. To keep up with its high-performance engine, the suspension, brakes, wheels, and tires were upgraded, too.

Vital Statistics

Callaway Camaro C-8

Production years: 1993–96
No. built: 73
Top speed: 172 mph (277 km/h)
Engine type: V8
Engine size: 6.3 liters, 404 hp
Cylinders: 8
Transmission: N/A
CO_2 emissions: N/A
EPA fuel economy ratings: N/A
Price: US$54,000

Dynamic design

The Callaway Camaro C-8 not only had better performance, it looked different, too. The Callaway CamAerobody kit was an aerodynamic design package created by Canadian car designer Paul Deutschman. Deutschman began designing with Callaway in the late 1980s. A true Callaway Camaro C-8 had to have both the performance and CamAerobody installed. The CamAerobody design only fits 1993–96 Camaros.

■ Callaway Camaro C-8s are rare vehicles.
There were only 55 SuperNatural Camaros
and 18 Callaway C-8s built from 1993 to 1996.

Reeves Callaway

Ely Reeves Callaway was born in Pennsylvania in 1947. He competed in—and won—the Formula Vee National Championship in 1970 and 1971. He also loved to work on car engines and started his own business in 1977 called Callaway Cars. Callaway took cars such as the Chevrolet Camaro and Corvette and installed aftermarket turbochargers that made them faster.

Picking up the pace

Chevrolet produced two pace cars during its fourth-generation span. The Camaro was chosen to pace the Indy 500 in 1993 and a stock car race called the Indianapolis Brickyard 400 in 1997. Stock car races are held on oval racetracks.

1993 Indy 500 pace car

In its debut year, Camaro's Z28 was given the honor of pacing the racecars for the Indy 500 held on May 30, 1993. It was the fourth time it had paced the famous car race.

The pace car's exterior was painted black-over-white—the top half being black and the bottom half and rims being white. Splitting the polar opposites was a band of colored ribbons: red, purple, yellow, and turquoise blue. The ribbons were tight around the car's nose, but appeared to be flowing loosely as they made their way around to the rear of the car.

30th anniversary

Camaro's 30th anniversary came in 1997. Chevrolet celebrated by releasing special edition, 30th Anniversary pace-car replicas.

This edition was a Camaro SS. It was painted white with broad orange racing stripes down the length of the nose and rear of the car. The interior came with black or white leather seats, with a houndstooth pattern in the center. This color combination was similar to the special edition Camaro SS that paced the Indy 500 in 1969. Americans liked the nod to the past, and scooped up 957 of them.

Special editions

Chevrolet offered a special edition Z28 pace car for buyers in 1993. These came in the same colors and had special decals to commemorate the race. The replica also featured the same color theme inside, with black and white seats and door panels, and ribbons flowing through them. In all, 663 replica Camaro pace cars were produced and sold.

The 1993 Indy pace Camaro had distinctive black and white bodywork with colored ribbons.

The end of the road

By 1996, Chevrolet executives felt that the Camaro had come to the end of its life. Few changes were made to the model in its last years. In 2002, the company announced that it was the end of the road for the popular sports car. On August 27, 2002, the last fourth-generation Camaro came off the assembly line.

SUV craze

SUV stands for Sport Utility Vehicle. SUVs became popular in North America in the 1990s. People with families usually bought them because they were roomier, and could seat up to seven people. Many felt they were safer to drive, too. The growing trend for Americans to drive larger, SUV-type vehicles is one of the reasons why Chevrolet discontinued the Camaro in 2002.

In the late 1990s, Chevrolet began responding to American's love of SUVs, producing vehicles such as the Tahoe.

A mystery decision

It is one of the great sports-car mysteries of the 1990s. High-performance, fourth-generation Camaros were leaving Mustangs in their dust. Camaros were a high-quality product, and everything about them was superb—handling, performance, and looks. They got better gas mileage than comparable Mustangs. They were even thousands of dollars cheaper than the Mustang. But still, the Ford Mustang was outselling the Camaro every year. In 1998, Chevrolet produced 54,026 Camaros compared to the 170,642 Mustangs sold by Ford. The worst year for Camaro sales was 2001, when only 29,009 were sold.

Farewell Camaro

The new SUV trend and decreasing sales meant the end of the 35-year-old Chevrolet pony car. Chevrolet gave Camaro fans one final goodbye edition—the 2002 SS 35th Anniversary. The red Camaro SS came with silver racing stripes that dissolved into checkered flags near the front and rear windows, and then turned solid again near the front and rear bumpers. The special edition came in convertible or T-top only. Even though it seemed like it might be Camaro's swan song, many hoped that the car would make a comeback in the near future.

The 35th Anniversary Camaro was available as a convertible or T-top.

Chapter 6

⟫ Camaro's Comeback ⟫⟫⟫⟫

It was hard to believe that after a 35-year run, an American sports car such as Camaro could really be gone for good. Many believed that Chevrolet would bring back the popular pony car and sure enough, after eight years of retirement, the Camaro came back bigger and better than ever.

Playing catch-up

GM decided to bring Camaro back for the same reason it had created the first one in 1967. Ford's new Mustang, released in 2005, was enjoying healthy sales. GM wanted in on the spoils and decided to jump into the pony car market once again.

A new concept

Concept cars are generally extreme in their style and design. Most **production cars** end up looking quite different than the concept they came from. But in Camaro's case, GM design and performance teams wanted to make the concept car as close to the production car as they could. Some of the best people in the car-design business got together to build a concept car.

GM put two design teams together to compete to see who could come up with the best design. One team was led by Corvette designer Tom Peters. Peters put Sangyup Lee in charge of his design team. Peters' team won the exterior design competition.

Sangyup Lee

Sangyup Lee was born in Korea. He did not grow up around American sports cars and never saw a Camaro until he was 20 years old. He moved to the U.S.A. and in 1995, he studied transportation design at the Art Center College of Design in Pasadena, California, graduating with honors in 1999. During his studies in California, Lee did *internships* at car companies such as Porsche.

Since its comeback, Camaro has seen various concept cars. This is called the Chroma.

Close to the Concept

Most concept cars give designers the freedom to take chances and experiment with style. But not so with the Camaro concept car. Designers were told to style the car into a concept that was very close to what the production vehicle would resemble.

Best in show

The new Camaro concept car was unveiled on January 8, 2006, at the North American International Auto Show held in Detroit. American car enthusiasts loved it straight away, and car magazine *AutoWeek* awarded it "Best in Show."

The 2006 Camaro concept car was greeted with enthusiasm by critics and the public alike.

Waiting in the wings

GM announced its plans to take the Camaro concept car to the production stage on August 10, 2006. To feed the growing interest in the car, they developed a Camaro convertible concept car, which they unveiled the following year, at the 2007 North American International Auto Show.

Retro style

Ford designers took styling cues from older Mustang models and redesigned them with a modern flare—creating a look that proved popular. Chevrolet design teams took the same approach and created the fifth-generation of Camaro based on the 1969 model.

Financial troubles

Production of the new Camaro was put off for another year due to financial troubles at GM. In the spring of 2009, the company was almost **bankrupt**. When the United States economy hit a **recession** in December 2007, many Americans were affected by rising prices and loss of jobs. GM employs millions of Americans. If the car company shut down, all these people would lose their jobs. To prevent this, the U.S. Congress voted to help GM out of its financial crisis by giving it billions of dollars from the Troubled Asset Relief Program.

The 2010 Camaro was the first time the car was offered with a sunroof.

Back to the 1960s

One of the designs borrowed from the 1969 Camaro was its front, inset, V-shaped grille. Another design similarity was the vents in front of the rear wheel fenders. The overall "Coke-bottle shape" that the first-generation Camaro was so well-known for returned as well. The new Camaro featured the same tucked-in waist in the middle of the car.

A star is born

In 2007, GM got a huge **marketing** boost for the upcoming Camaro. Millions of people would see it in a starring role in the upcoming movie *Transformers* as the Autobot named Bumblebee. The character of Bumblebee disguises himself as a yellow Camaro.

Two sequel *Transformer* movies followed. Each was a huge box-office success that brought in millions of dollars. The advertising also helped Chevrolet sell the new generation of Camaros!

In the movie *Transformers*, Bumblebee uses his small size and agility to deliver messages and spy for the Autobots under the leadership of Optimus Prime.

Not a beetle

In the original *Transformers* story, Bumblebee is actually a yellow Volkswagen Beetle. For the 2007 trilogy of films, director Michael Bay decided to change the car because it reminded him too much of the 1968 Disney movie car, Herbie, from *The Love Bug!* The new Camaro—in yellow with black racing stripes—got the role instead!

Transforming the Camaro

For each *Transformers* movie, special edition Bumblebee Camaros were created. In 2007, they were based on the concept car design. For 2010, Chevrolet offered a limited edition Bumblebee Camaro that resembled the one in *Transformers: Revenge of the Fallen*. The Rally Yellow car had black rally stripes inside the hood bulge. It also came with Autobot fender badges and wheel caps.

In 2012, another *Transformers* special edition came out. The Bumblebee package comes with Rally Yellow paint and black racing stripes that hug the outsides of the bulging hood. It also comes with Autobot Shield logos on the wheel center caps and the inside headrests.

The yellow paint and black stripes marked out the Bumblebee models.

Finally...

With a healthy boost of advertising from the *Transformer* movies, the American public could hardly wait to get their hands on a fifth-generation Camaro. They finally got their chance in April 2009, when the 2010 Camaro could be purchased by anyone who could afford the base price of US$23,530.

Welcome back

In its returning year, the Camaro came in coupe form only. The base model, LS, came with a 3.6-liter V6 engine offering 304 hp. The Camaro could also be purchased in an SS high-performance model. Six-speed manual transmission Camaro SSs came with a standard 6.2-liter V8 engine with 426 hp. Not too shabby for a street-legal vehicle!

Made in Canada, again

The fifth-generation of Camaro was once again made in Canada. This time they were made at a GM assembly plant in Oshawa, Ontario. This plant uses a new robotic, flexible assembly system that saves on energy and can produce more vehicles. It was also rated one of the best assembly plants in North America in terms of vehicle quality!

Camaros are assembled at the General Motors plant in Oshawa, Canada.

Active Fuel Management

In 2010, Chevrolet Camaros came with Active Fuel Management systems. This conserves fuel during times when less power is needed, such as when cruising on highways. The car's computer senses that less fuel is needed and shuts off half the **cylinders**. In a Camaro SS V8, the vehicle ran on four cylinders instead of the full eight.

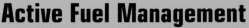
2010 Camaro SS

Production year: 2010
No. built: 70,169
Top speed: 155 mph (250 km/h)
Engine type: V8
Engine size: 6.2 liters, 426 hp
Cylinders: 8
Transmission: 6-speed automatic or manual
CO_2 emissions: 468 gpm
EPA fuel economy ratings: 16 mpg (city); 25 mpg (highway)
Price: US$31,795

■ The 2010 Camaro SS was a high-performance model with a 6.2-liter V8 engine.

🏁 AMAZING FACTS

Speed police

Fifth-generation Camaros cannot go faster than 155 mph (250 km/h). The car's computer automatically shuts off fuel supply to the engine when the car reaches this speed.

SS special editions

If starring in its own blockbuster movies wasn't enough, the 2010 Camaro convertible SS was also given the honor of pacing the Indy 500's 100th anniversary race in 2011. The Camaro SS pace car edition was white with the famous Hugger Orange racing stripe down the center of the car from grille to back bumper—the same color combination used in the 1969 pace car edition. A 2011 Camaro Convertible Indy 500 pace car replica was made available to the public.

2010 Synergy Series

The Camaro Synergy Series is an annual appearance package that was produced from 2010. The first Camaro Synergy Special Edition could be purchased for an LT coupe model Camaro only, and was painted Synergy Green with Cyber Gray rally stripes. Only 2,425 Synergy Camaros were produced.

Honor and Valor

A limited edition Camaro called the Honor and Valor can only be purchased by those who have actively served in the U.S. Army, Navy, Air Force, Marines, or Coast Guard. The package can only be applied to the Camaro SS, and comes in three color choices: black, red, or white. It also comes with special Honor and Valor badges with a yellow ribbon that shows support for American troops.

■■➡

The color scheme used on the Camaro pace cars for the Indy 500's 100th anniversary reflected that of the 1969 pace cars.

2011 Synergy Series

The 2011 Camaro Synergy Special Edition had more choices and was available in LT or SS models, in coupe or convertible form. The package could be added to any Camaro in black, white, or red. Even though there were more choices, fewer than 400 were made.

2012 Synergy Series

The 2012 Synergy Special Edition Camaro SS convertible has a Silver Ice exterior with black synergy stripes. It began as a concept car at the 2009 SEMA (Specialty Equipment Market Association) to show off Camaro's accessories and parts that changed the look of the car.

The Synergy Special LT was painted in a vivid "Synergy Green."

Camaro kudos

Even when it seemed like Chevrolet's Camaro had come to an end, the popular American sports car made a movie-star comeback, and showed the world that it was definitely not ready to retire. The new generation of Camaro is better than ever, and fuel efficient to boot. And Camaro keeps looking forward—the 2013 Camaro ZL1 convertible will be Chevy's most powerful convertible ever.

■ The future of Camaro – the speedy 2012 ZL1.

Fastest Camaro ever

The 2012 ZL1 is the fastest production Camaro ever made by Chevrolet. This speed demon comes with a 6.2-liter supercharged V8 engine that gives it 580 hp and an *acceleration* of 0–100 mph (0–161 km/h) in less than ten seconds!

Camaro's legacy

Each of the five generations of Chevrolet Camaro reflect the economy, energy and environmental issues, and car-buying trends of its time. At the start, the Camaro was a pony car created to take a bite out of Ford Mustang's sales. Today, with its new movie-star status and awesome performance record, Camaro drivers view Mustangs in their rear-view mirrors. It has been a long road for Camaro.

Long live Camaro

Camaro celebrated its 45th anniversary in 2012 with an anniversary edition, which made its first appearance at the Camaro5 Fest II in Arizona on April 15, 2011. This beauty boasts black leather seats that have special 45th anniversary logos and red, white, and blue stitching.

Club Camaro

The American Camaro Association is a club for Camaro owners, collectors, and enthusiasts. They oversee over 150 different Camaro clubs throughout North America. Different regional clubs organize meetings, car shows, rides, and other group events. Members share advice about restoring their cars.

Camaro Timeline

1964   Ford releases the Mustang

1966   Three 1967 Camaro models go on sale—the Sport Coupe and the upgraded Super Sport (SS) and Rally Sport (RS) packages

1967   Camaro paces the Indianapolis 500

1969   Camaro ZL-1 is released

1970   The first car of the second-generation—the 1970½—is released

1973   The Camaro SS is discontinued; oil crisis causes problems for automakers; new emissions standards are set by the EPA

1974   Maximum Speed Law comes into effect, setting the speed limit at 55 mph (89 km/h); the Z28 is used in the IROC race

1977   Camaro reinvents the Z28; Camaro outsells the Mustang for the first time

1979   The LT Camaro is renamed the Berlinetta

1981   The Z28 becomes the first Camaro to have Computer Command Control

1982   The third-generation hits the market; the cross-fire injection system is offered in Camaros

1984   The 1984 Camaro sets sales records for the third-generation

1985   The IROC package is introduced as an upgrade to the Z28

1987   Camaro's Norwood, Ohio, plant closes and production is focussed at the Van Nuys plant; Camaro celebrates its 25th anniversary

1988   The 1LE package is available to those buyers who can figure out how to get hold of it

1989   Jim Perkins takes over as general manager of Chevrolet

1990   Camaro loses the rights to the IROC-Z name and reverts to Z28

1992   Camaro releases a 25th anniversary edition; end of the third-generation

1993   Production moves to Canada; fourth-generation Camaros are accused of looking too much like a Japanese import but praised for performance and handling; the first Callaway Camaro is produced

1996   The SS model makes a comeback

1997   Camaro paces the Indianapolis Brickyard 400; 30th anniversary edition is released

2001   Camaro experiences its worst sales year

2002   Production of all Camaros ceases

2006   A new Camaro concept car is unveiled at the North American International Auto Show in Detroit

2007   Camaro stars in the new *Transformers* movie

2009   The fifth-generation goes on sale to the American public

2010   Limited edition Bumblebee Camaro is released

2011   Camaro paces the Indy 500's 100th anniversary race

2012   Another *Transformers* special edition is produced; 45th anniversary edition is released

Further Information

Books

Camaro White Book 1967–2011
by Mike Antonick
(Michael Bruce Associates, Inc., 2011)

Camaro: Five Generations of Performance
by Darwin Holmstrom
(Motorbooks, 2006)

Websites

http://history.gmheritagecenter.com/wiki/index.php/Some_Camaro_History
A history of Camaro from the GM Heritage Center

www.edmunds.com/chevrolet/camaro/history.html
A brief history of Camaro from the used car website

www.camaros.org/geninfo.shtml
A series of questions and answers about Camaro

Glossary

acceleration A measure of how quickly something speeds up

aerodynamic Describing something with a low amount of drag

aftermarket A car that has been altered, or changed, by another company

appearance package A version of a car that is produced to look particularly good, with special paintwork and other decorative details

automatic transmission A device that shifts a car's gears without help from the driver according to the speed it is traveling

bankrupt When a company or individual runs out of money

catalytic converter A device attached to a car's exhaust system that changes harmful emissions to less-harmful emissions

concept car A vehicle made to show the public a new design or technology

convertible A car with a top that can be put up or taken down

coupe A hard-topped sports car with two doors

customized Changed to meet a particular person's needs or preferences

cylinders The chambers in an engine in which the piston moves

durable Strong and long-lasting

embargo A governmental law that does not allow trade with a specific country

emissions In a vehicle, the toxic fumes that the engine produces and releases into the air

executives People in a governing, or management, position at a company

grille The front screen of a vehicle that usually sits between the headlights

horsepower (hp) The amount of pulling power an engine has based on the number of horses it would take to pull the same load

internship A training program where students learn skills while on the job

manual transmission A device that a driver must operate to shift a car's gears

marketing Promoting a product to try and sell it

modifications Alterations to something to make it suit a particular purpose

performance package A version of a car that has been enhanced from the base model so that it has greater power

platform On a vehicle, the base or frame on which a vehicle is built

pony cars Sporty two-door cars with high performance

production cars Cars that are made in large numbers on an assembly line

recession A period of time when the economy is not doing well

replica A reproduction, or copy, of an original

suspension A system of springs that protects the chassis of a car

turbochargers Gas compressors in the engine that make a vehicle go faster

urethane A type of plastic that is especially tough and is often used as a protective coating

Index

Entries in **bold** indicate pictures